SOMERSET IN PHOTOGRAPHS

RICH WILTSHIRE

AMBERLEY

Amberley Publishing
The Hill, Stroud
Gloucestershire, GL5 4EP

www.amberley-books.com

Copyright © Rich Wiltshire, 2019

The right of Rich Wiltshire to be identified as the Author of this work has been
asserted in accordance with the Copyrights, Designs and Patents Act 1988.

ISBN 978 1 4456 8569 4 (print)
ISBN 978 1 4456 8570 0 (ebook)

British Library Cataloguing in Publication Data.
A catalogue record for this book is available from the British Library.

Typesetting by Aura Technology and Software Services, India.
Printed in the UK.

ACKNOWLEDGEMENTS

I would firstly like to say a big thanks to Amberley Publishing for all their support in creating this wonderful book. Secondly, I would like to say a big thanks to all my friends and family who have stood by me throughout my journey as a photographer.

I would also like to thank Canon, Kase Filters and Gitzo Tripods for the support with the equipment that I use.

ABOUT THE PHOTOGRAPHER

I am a photographer based in the town of Bridgwater, Somerset, and have been a landscape photographer for seven years. I got into photography after an accident stopped me working as a builder. I have always been a keen photographer, but more point and shoot. After the accident I was diagnosed with depression and anxiety due to not been able to work, so I decided to pursue photography further and learn the fundamentals, as well as how to use a camera to its full potential. This really helped me through some difficult times, giving me a purpose and a focus in life. Since then I have won or come runner-up in various awards: runner-up in Landscape Image of the Year 2017 with the Photo Guild, winner of two international competitions with Viewbug, winner of Month Landscape competition with Shoot the Frame, as well as winning various local contests. I have also worked with the BBC and have had work published and featured in a variety of magazines worldwide.

Website: www.rgw-photography.co.uk
Facebook: @RichWiltshirePhotography (RGW-Photography)
Instagram: @rich_wiltshire_photography
Email: contact@rgw-photography.co.uk

INTRODUCTION

Somerset is one of the most diverse and rural counties in England and includes the rolling Blackdown, Mendip and Quantock hills, Exmoor National Park, and large flat expanses of land including the Somerset Levels. This diversity has been transformative to capture.

The images I have used in the book have taken me around three years to collect, as often you can go out and, even with planning, be set back by obstacles such as last-minute weather changes. What I love about landscape photography is that it gives me the chance to discover all these beautiful places I would never have known about before taking it up.

My favourite place in Somerset has to be Kilve Beach as I love the rugged coastline and how it continues to change with the tides. I also love to photograph Glastonbury as it is such a mystical place, especially in the fog. My favourite time of day to photograph is the golden hour before sunset as the light is soft and creates a beautiful glow over the countryside.

I hope the images in this book are an example to people all over the country of just how beautiful our area really is, and I also hope they inspire like-minded people to go out and explore for themselves the rugged, natural wonder that is Somerset.

SPRING

The rising sun, Ham Wall

Bath Abbey in the rain

Bridgwater Dock

Broomfield overlooking Bridgwater

Batheaston

Birnbeck sunset

Brean Down from above

Sunset at the estuary, River Brue, Burnham-on-Sea

Bridgwater at high tide

Castle Bridge, Stogursey

Clevedon sunset

Coastal views at Kilve

Huntspill Beacon

Kilve coastline

Taunton School

Pulteney Bridge

Orchard Portman

Somerset coast, Kilve

Spring colours, Bridgwater

Rainbow over the Somerset Levels

Sowing the seeds, Nether Stowey

St Audries Bay

Triscombe Manor

Watchet Harbour Lighthouse at sunset

Wells Cathedral at sunset

SUMMER

Quantock Hills

The heart of Clevedon

Minehead

Beach huts, Weston-super-Mare

Chew Valley Lake

Beacon Hill views

Burnham-on-Sea

Berrow groynes at sunset

Bridgwater Canal

Clevedon Pill at sunset

Berrow Church

Grounded wreck, River Brue

Driftwood Café, Weston-super-Mare

Enmore fog

SS *Nornen* wreck, Berrow

Haystacks, Dipford

Huntworth

Lilstock observation tower

Kilve sunset

Portishead sunset

Misty wood, Compton Dundon

Blagdon Lake

Orchard Portman fields

Norton Dam, Norton Fitzwarren

Rickford during the golden hour

Sand Bay

Robin Hood's Hut, Goathurst

WWT Steart Marshes

Swan Lake, Plainsfield

The Hide

The bridge, Dunster Castle

West Lydford

Stolford at high tide

Summer corn, West Monkton

Grand Pier, Weston-super-Mare

Nether Stowey

AUTUMN

The Royal Crescent, Bath

Vicars' Close, Wells

Morning stroll, Burrow Mump

Autumn colours at Broomfield

Boat & Anchor, Bridgwater

Autumn at Selworthy

Birnbeck Pier, Weston-super-Mare

Abandoned boat, River Brue

Dunster Castle

City of Bath

Glastonbury Tor fog

Glastonbury Tor

Kings Cliff, Bridgwater

Grounded boat, River Brue

Hawkridge sunset

The copse, Broomfield

Periwinkle Cottage, Selworthy

Quantock horses

River Barle, Dulverton

The Circus, Bath

River Tone, Taunton

Combe Sydenham Hall

The tree at Orchard Portman

Triscombe Manor

WINTER

Clatworthy Resevoir

Bossington Beach

Rainbow over Aston Windmill, Chapel Allerton

Dunkery

Beached boat, Porlock Weir

Ashford Reservoir Tower

Compton Bishop

Gorge Waterfall, Cheddar

Burnham-on-Sea Lighthouse

Burrow Mump river reflections

Crook Peak

Burrowbridge river walk

Crowcombe in the mist

French Weir at sunset

Ham Hill

Millennium Maze, Kilve Court

Kilve Beach sunset

Helwell Bay

King Alfred's Tower, Brewham

Montacute House drive

Light on the Quantock Hills

Lost in the Quantock Hills

Ditcheat

Glastonbury rising above the fog

River Tone, Bathpool

Somerset Levels

Three swans, Burrow Mump

St Audries in the snow

Trull Waterfall

The Hide, Bridgwater Bay

Ham Wall reflections

Ingleborough Tower Windmill, Walton

Wells Cathedral

Wicker cathedral

Glastonbury full moon